A GLANCE WILL TELL YOU & A DREAM CONFIRM

by

TOM MAC INTYRE

DEDALUS

Dublin

The Dedalus Press
24 The Heath,
Cypress Downs,
Dublin 6W
Ireland
22/3/95

ISBN 1 873790 58 9 (paper)
ISBN 1 873790 59 7 (bound)

Cover: "Icon Blue" by Catriona O'Connor

ACKNOWLEDGEMENTS
These poems have been previously published in *element*, *Force 10*, *Fortnight*, *Ireland of the Welcomes*, *Krino*, *The Poetry Ireland Review*, *Dedalus Irish Poets*, *The Honest Ulsterman*, *The Irish Review*, *The University Review*, and *Windows*.
The collection was readied for submission in the comfort of *The Heinrich Böll Cottage on Achill Island*; the author extends thanks to all associated with that project.

Dedalus Press Books are represented and distributed abroad by Password, 23 New Mount St., Manchester M4 4DE.

The Dedalus Press receives financial assistance from An Chomhairle Ealaíon, The Arts Council, Ireland.

CONTENTS

for Felicity Wellbeloved

PROFESSION

The grandmother caught
the red gansy's flit
turning the lane,

got there in time
to see it melt
the next turn, let

out a roar, salted,
put down the boot,
did sums, found him

in The Hill Field,
easy as skip, hold-
ing a calf by the tail ...

She knew then, she
always claimed after :
cut of the child,

calf nose in the air,
July day an oven.
Back to a sycamore,

she watched from the shade.

ARTIST & MODEL

'You are becoming
more and more
like the drawings ... '

The line is one
with her prehensile eye,
I view the drawings
I may not deny,
they enter, they inform,
more and more
I am becoming
like the drawings ...

I feel – multiplied.
I feel rapport
with all endangered species.

'In what orchard
were you born?'

That open gaze.
She reaches again
for paper, crayon.
My clothes fly off –

I've no idea
where this'll end.

HOOF-TAPS

Banished for years
the horse opens
my door again,

and I'm afraid,
fear those hooves,
fear that fecund breath

while, insouciantly
as an old lover,
he makes bold, fondles
me to recognition
of pure betrothal –

Say your prayers
by The Wet Gate;
drink, savour;
turn your face
to The Gates of The Sea.

BILLET-DOUX

I've made a search
over quite some time
for the poem which moves
towards certain lines
found on the road
or dreaming, maybe; I
dedicate them to you,
Formidable One, where-
ever you breathe, you
coming to me under
leaf-light or early star,

your pillow the earth
and breasts of the fair.

YOU

Tying your hair behind
or hovering to kiss
or caught in the window
fringe hiding your eyes,

you're a mover, sway
like the one
tip-top of the tree
and licked by the sun ...

I remember that kiss,
light wand of lips.

– *What bird owns The May?*

I glimpse you again.
I'll gather your name.

PIANISSIMO

the child of grace
greets her weather,
on hair, on face,
shoulders, breast,
still benediction
of powdery snow

to the smiling one
who trims his beard
with idle hand,
whose lap gathers
the fine fall

to first of your kisses
bestowed while I sleep,
sound of a kiss,
promise of kisses ...

Suddenly I know
Death is a mountain.

SUN-BATHING

There'd been several approaches,
all the same a surprise
when this time the sparrow
zipped from the apple-tree
to land on the tip
of my big toe. A first
for me, can't speak for the bird.

We looked at each other –
a casual sort of hello,
shy at that, gregariously modest :
Au revoir – and the sparrow's
enjoying the warm shade
of a thicket convenient.

I lay in the sun.
Thought of you.
May it happen again.

69

My anus juices
like the grape,
tongue and teeth
I tell flavours,
the room smells
of the forest floor.

'There was a book
owned a tall
book-case of my childhood –
Girl of the Limberlost',

she inclines
a verdant eye,
'Never read it,
no one read it'.

Good steady pace
a red thread
travels the wall
above the mantelpiece.

'*Girl of the Limberlost*.
Cover could've been
ash-blue or dove-grey
or, could be, maroon'.

The book drifts
from shelf to shelf.
'How're you doing?'

Her belly smiles,
the book-case gleams,
we lie there
deep in clover.

KISSES

Would you like to hear
of the kisses we share?

Track of The Sanderlings,
Hide-and-Seek of The Swallow,
Yellow-Hammer-And-Tongs,

Tit's Morning Milk,
Linnet Reflecting, Sweet
Sleep of The Thrush,

Swift Going South, Take
Your Fill of The Thermal,
Streak of The Kingfisher,
Golden Plovers Wheel The Shore –

nights like tonight,
Lord, how they play,
as The Summer Triangle
folds The Milky Way.

SKINNY-DIP, 4am

Breast-stroke, naturally,
back-stroke, side,
dolphin, butterfly,

this is the one stream,
rapids here of watered silk,
I coast declivities, own
a blessed basin,
blessed descend
to the one spring,

tease a way, delicate
does it, part
fold on fold,
lisp within,
listen, a pulse –

o taste and see –
full-fathomed be –
and hug the undertow :

unison and only daughter
we round a curve
where I drop to sleep,
moon a shoe
that my star fits
high in the southern sky.

AT THE THEATRE

Look at you, speaking
and laughing too loudly
and plying the hands
in bleak semaphore,

I agree, *ma jolie*,
at a generous stretch
we could touch, having touched
talk, smile and such
but we can't,
so we don't,

I watch you, intent,
watching the play
we're not watching while
the play we watch
sings like a bird –

Our bodies met
like famished things;
as for our souls,
our souls brushed wings,

how you listen,
believer turned infidel,
weight of your listening,

already I can tell
you'll leave at the interval.

RSVP

Urbanely leppin'
out of his skin,
frog wonders would
I care to dine?
Cucumber sandwiches,
pears, prickly or plain,
table-cloth sap-green
of the pendent world.

'I'm the one', says
frog's bright eyes, 'or
have you forgotten?
Amn't I the one
who laid it down,
No need for hammer
in the rainy season'.

DECADE OF THE LISTENING EARS

I've heard them groan
and seen them weep,
one there was, ebullient,
laughed when entered,

some for counsel came,
more for exercise,
droves for divilment,
a clutch to make amends,

now and then
the one who brings
the kiss just ripened
on her tree of longing

but she who haunts me,
for whom they swear
I'm wickedly to blame,
she speaks another bounty,

she is the journey
and journey delayed,
bliss of encounter,
cost of the road.

MARCH, ERRISLANNIN

Jupiter minding The Twins,
Venus blithe in the west,
my love yawns, reclines,
'Weight of desire', she says –

that suffices,
the house capsizes;

vernal now
the curlew's cry,
vernal find us
where we lie.

COMMENCEMENT NOTES

Burn to shiver be your weather.

Chariot without the wheel-rim,
we call poetry, and then,
Wheel-rim without the chariot;

among the letters – pause,
defer – imperious *S*
is chatelaine and courtesan;

our vision mushrooms laze
under water, amorous –
learn the pool's quiet;

dancing is how to breathe,
wear the berried sprig
the dancer's step implies.

COMPANION

Slip ashore, show
you how to gather
pollen, simple breath,

music wishing
to be born
loops the page,

a red sea-rod
knows every fish
wise in the lap

of your ninth wave,
wave in waiting
shy to the west,

it's long past noon,
the night comes on,
down to the water,

child of nature,
down to the water,
play me home.

HH

Trouble with High Horse
it's by definition a gallop
plus, world well knows,
Herr High Horse owns
the original patent-leather
life-guaranteed (thereafter
to heirs and/or assignees)
intractable mouth :
                                        further,
don't ask for comfort
up there, ground's honest
crust is far far away,
close your eyes, Mister,
we're talkin' cordal whiplash,
whirrs, blue migraine,
and the dart malign,

public stare, of course
they stare, stare and smile,
heigh-ho your elevation,
their sweet event, subject/
object/abject, of curiosity,
ridicule, piquancies of scorn,

still the bastard gallops,
you smell Casualty Ward,
you smell worse, smell
de mortuis speak-easy,
man in the black coat,
man in the white, tile,
trolley, the feral bell,

a woman once loved
(where do they come from
and how do they know?),
consummate seat, cosy inside
of those opulent knees,
mount joy to behold,
appears just to disappear,
tandem furlong, she peels
off to the left, WAVES,
consigns me, *quelle biche*,
to drink it alone,
enter now the walled town

of atrocious memory,
High Horse halts, smoothly
agrees to sixteen hands,
nibbles, nonchalant, and I'm
on mother ground again,

mustering, even in this
parsimonious hour, remnant
poise; citizenry about,
male, female, riding gear,
a sense that I'm expected,
rather as if they know
all or a good deal

more than I am like to,
the young woman solicitous
out of all the stories
approaches – have we met? –
offers, slender fingers,
that small white pill
out of all the stories :
froideur the word, I
take, turn away, ditch.

What now for recreation?
Try Pensive-stroke-the-chin,
the welcome-party's vanishing –
a knot of reservations,
fine, fine, fine, fine,
I too have mine,

the silence rages,
they'd a synod here
in the Middle Ages
that solved nothing,
since, still water –
Like Picasso, we
insist on discussing
only religious questions –
man on a tea-chest
at no one's behest,

the horse sidles up,
trots, rather, dainty trot,
the stirrups sway divination,
and the fucker waits,
licking his chops
and ticking his tots,

unmeltable
dreamery-creamery butter
the key and the lock
of his round-the-clock
mulberry bilberry blackberry sigh.

APRIL MISCELLANY

Cuckoo's bell
assures the gullible
all is well,

finches swop
deliquescent
sighs of green

and the pied wagtails –
Okay, let's do it –
are off to a party

(meadow-pipit
disconsolate at
the entire arrangement),

very first swallow's
a touch-me-not,
twig in mouth

starling's ruminant,
stonechat bangs
pebble on pebble,

and should prevail,
and may prevail,
but cormorant

is rock and sky
and shall prevail :
salute at once

the bracingly
heraldic stance –
poised oval

against sea-silver,
winsome thrapple
of the unappeasable,

Corvus marinus
at your service,
unwinking one

who works alone,
belly and lance
in perfect tune;

often we meet
as I walk the sunset,
a focussed line

high overhead, I
like to imagine
nod as he passes –

We'll find an hour –
that tilt, no way
pushy, not unfriendly,

sonsy April's
cool imperative
and evening air.

A GLANCE WILL TELL YOU AND A DREAM CONFIRM

The White One
starts the central ridge,
The Hag ends it,

she sits between
you and the sea.
Landward

a ridge abuts,
The Black Boar
kindly points a route,

here Derryclare,
The Two Corries, The Height
The Soldier Fell;

other bits, pieces,
The Goat, The Speckled,
somebody's Testicle,

away north
The Bald Man,
south The Spewy Slopes

enhance the road.
The peaks glisten,
rain or shine.

Climb, traveller,
or stiffen slowly
on the plain.

NOCTIS EQUI

Lost road. Thick of dusk.
It was no great surprise.
Reared. Gallop. And gone.

House entered, sign given,
simple the measure
of sweet visitation.

All green, untutored green,
breath and limb and well-
spring of the morning.

THIS EVENTFUL LIFE

Another point. They're level.
The gifted midfielder –
bit excitable –
clouts his marker
twice across the face.

Spectacled, cap
on the Kildare side,
Mr Punctilious
notes the offender's name,
issues the warning.

And the spectator
wakes to a nosebleed,
red on the pillow,
dishevelled posy
from the wide beyond.

EQUESTRIAN STATUE

How could it ever work?
I'm flesh and blood, mate,
breather, feeder, I shit,
sweat, itch, sleep and wake.

Your press-gang, noble
warriors all, were steeped;
as for the fozy General,
he's poxed to be alive.

Some, no doubt, will plead
it had its funny side,
frankly, I don't see it,
nor, I imagine, do you,
maybe no one does,
maybe it wasn't funny.

Anyway, when I found you
holed up in the stable
(you knew the rendezvous),
when I duly surfaced
as my verifiable self,
white pony of middle
years and honest bent,

the best of your endeavour
was one hand the little
bit of tenderness, other,
other anybody's guess,

I felt free to leave
(and noted the door
closed on my heels) :
you come and find me.

PRESTISSIMO INDOORS

Breath of purple
on your markings

holds me still,
brims surmise;

informed strangers
watch as I admire

beak and claws,
temper fret, weigh

invitation :
motionless

on the table-corner
you don't look towards,

don't look away,
dispense for signature

blast of heat
from the tumbling core.

PANGUR EILE

Within my dream
I watch you sleeping,
am shown your dream,

my eyes widen
to a cat couchant,
snake for piping,

cool periphery,
head and tail
meeting by the cat's

tail, on the cat's
head a small bird,
I take my fill

of this picture, pray
it may endure,
it has more to do,

the cat couchant
is first to go,
next the piping,

the snake sloughs
itself, the bird's left,
the bird dissolves

to just the head,
head to an eye,
the eye holds

mine, the eye's gone;
still dreaming, I rouse
you from sleep

to tell – everything,
that in my dream
I watched you sleeping –

your eyes widen –
saw your dream,
how it played

there – all the keys,
and lightest touch,
you hold me close

(that bird's eye),
hold me, hold me,
we continue sleeping.

AISLING GHEAL

The one-strand river
never looked better,
pleasure-bound
the coral cove,
the quiet's in love,

two pup-seals dandle
slack of the tide,
breast-to-breast splash
each other, all comers,
jap me with beginning,
middle, end, shout –

Fall into the milk
and spend your luck.
The night will come
you'll give us suck.

A beat. Centuries.
I find a whisper,
the whisper carries
life and limb –

Yours be mine
the time to play.
Mine be yours
the time to swim.

FIELD OBSERVATIONS ON THE CRAW CREE

Set paper on fire,
then place in jar.
Apply to the chest.
Pull free. Wait for
an echoing report.

If the cure works,
it was the *craw cree*,
and no mistake;
if the cure doesn't,
you've something else.

Concerning the words :
craw cree is frequent;
cree craw thrives
also, familiar variant.

This afflicition
is due to a bone
pressing upon the heart.

MANY WHILE PLAYING

Europa, Persephone,
had no need
of amphetamines,

some for flowers,
more for curls,
spill your pearls,
eat the world –

O, the bagel-babies
of my salad days
and green enjambments –

let's gather bog-myrtle,
doss above on the hill,
and Wistful, heed well,

if you don't see a star-wheel,
the star-wheels shine still.

SMALL HOURS

The red cat knows
and lets you know
everybody knows

nothing open
two in the morning
except legs.

That's why she's here;
besides, she's got
squatter's rights.

Don't stare –
her bloodless red's
tricky to breathe –

where are you, love,
at the other
end of my tether?

The red cat waits,
could wait forever.
All she wants

is liver and lights
when you say *when*
and not till then.

A bientôt.
The red cat melts,
furls to afterglow.

A bientôt.

THE INTENDED

She released a look
that stripped me,

first of three
looks of a lifetime;

of those to come
one will embrace,

the other boldly
bear us away.

AVIARY

Spirit-birds love
black of the bog,
banks loaded,
juice on the spade,

from nowhere gather
in celebration,
taste the action,
call it home.

You venture close :
pacey echoes
stir and murmur
names forgone,

Whimbrel, Whinchat,
Grebe, Merganser,
the names don't fit
quite, the birds mind

their own business,
a heron shows,
lifts, departs,
you've met before,

that's the hero
nicked your cap
and will not, will not
give it back ...

***

While in The Park
where leaf and bough
hum cultivation,
the walks cursive

and the ponds advised,
behold them horny,
loose in the hilts,
I want it now –

she stalls, stunned,
kindled, candle-coy,
the cock belts for
the cunt *en fleur*,

buccaneer swoop,
aboard, she gives,
subsides, they solder
perigee and apogee,

The Park trembles,
firms aplomb,
defines with tact
The Probation Act.

* * *

The wood at dusk.
Attend the scutch-grass.
Scatter of jackdaws
down in the mouth.

Camouflage rags
and ponger helmets
process in silence,
halt under a beech.

Artillery resounds.
Where's the front?
The heron glides in,
tucks the wings.

'Never a barrage
that didn't lift'.
All for peace
you nod assent.

Swish of rockets.
Someone's for it.
Goodman Heron
scans his squaddies –

'The sooty pongers
are a lovely touch'.